Books by Richard Howard

Poetry

FELLOW FEELINGS *1976*

TWO-PART INVENTIONS *1974*

FINDINGS *1971*

UNTITLED SUBJECTS *1969*

THE DAMAGES *1967*

QUANTITIES *1962*

Criticism

ALONE WITH AMERICA *1969*

PREFERENCES *1974*

Fellow Feelings

FELLOW FEELINGS

Poems by *Richard Howard*

New York *Atheneum* 1976

The poems have been previously published as follows:

DECADES *in American Review No. 22, February 1975*

RANDALL JARRELL *in Modern Poetry Studies, Vol. IV, No. 2, Autumn 1973*

THE ASSIGNATION WITH VALERY LARBAUD *in The Ohio Review, Vol. XVI, Fall 1974*

AGAIN FOR HEPHAISTOS *in The Ohio Review, Vol. XVI, Fall 1974*

AUDIENCES *in The Harvard Advocate, Spring 1975*

VENETIAN INTERIOR, 1889 *in The Georgia Review, Vol. XXIX, Spring 1975*

HOWARD'S WAY *in Ploughshares, Autumn 1975*

COMPULSIVE QUALIFICATIONS *in Poetry (Chicago, June 1973 & 1975)*

SEMI-PRIVATE *in The Columbia Forum, Vol. II, Winter 1973*

PERSONAL VALUES *in Shenandoah, Vol. XXIV, Fall 1972*

AND SO THE PRINCE OBSCURED HIS CONTEMPLATION *in Shenandoah, Vol. XXII, Summer 1971*

FROM THE FILES OF THE SECRET POLICE *in Partisan Review, Vol. XXXVIII No. 3, 1971*

THE COMEDY OF ART *in Antaeus, No. 10, Summer 1973*

CLOSET DRAMA *in A Joseph Cornell Album, ed. Dore Ashton, Viking Press, 1974*

PURGATORY, FORMERLY PARADISE *in The Georgia Review, Vol. XXX Fall 1975*

DISCARDED *and* VOCATIONAL GUIDANCE *in American Poetry Review, February 1976.*

Library of Congress Cataloging in Publication Data
I. Title.   PS3515.08415F4   *1976*   811'.5'4
75–34063   ISBN *0–689–10705–6*

for Sanford Friedman

I

II

III

(I)

Decades

for Hart Crane

1   *Crane's Canary Cottage.*   I have turned four,
and the tablecloth between my mother and me
(my father opposite, of course) invites
pollution of its pure canary note
by a nest of shiny knives and glasses—"not
for fingering." This is my first meal *out*
and I must behave, on my father's sharp orders
and yours—your father's: it is their bill of fare
we pay for, and who knew how much it cost,

that April evening as we ate? My mother
ate my father, her leftovers mine till now:
I failed like yours—your father—to defend
myself against the opposite sex, my own,
that night the news came, Mother's Day for sure,
that April something, nineteen thirty-two,
when Wheelwright said you turned to *Fish Food* (he
turned it to advantage in the very first
of all your elegies, asking final questions:

*what did you see as you fell, what did you hear
as you sank?*).   I fed to find the answers, for
that was a sacramental feast. Dear Hart,
our mothers ate our fathers, what do we
eat but each other? All the things we take
into our heads to do! and let strange creatures
make our mouths their home. Our problem is not
to find who remembers our parents—our problem is
to find who remembers ourselves. I love our problem,

it becomes our solution: unbecoming, it dissolves.
I was four, you drowned. Now you remember me.

1

II   *Laukhuff's Bookstore.*   I am fourteen, I live
on the Diet of Words, shoving a ladder around
high shelves while the German ex-organ-maker
smokes with a distant nightmare in his eyes
("You have heard of Essen," he murmurs, "you never
will again": it is nineteen forty-three),
his body on hinges, his elbows hovering wide
over the *Jugendstil* bindings (Werfel, Kraus . . .)
like a not-quite-open penknife. "Hart Crane?

He came here to marry the world . . . You understand?
Maritare mundum: it is the work of magic,
Mirandola says it somewhere, to marry the world . . .
And not much time to do it in, he had
to read all the books, to marry, *then* to burn . . .
It is one kind of greatness to grow old—
to be *able* to grow old, like Goethe;
it was Hart's kind to refuse. You understand?"
Laukhuff is asking *me*, laughing through smoke

his postponing, renouncing laugh. No, I don't—
that much I do. I climb down, clutching *The Bridge*
and hand it over. "Will I understand this,
Mr Laukhuff? Should I buy it?" "Cross it first.
You won't, but there is a certain value, there is
poetic justice in the sense of having missed
the full meaning of things. Sure, buy it. Spend
all you have, your mother will give you more."
The German penknife closes with a click.

Marriage, Hart. The endless war. The words.
Cleveland was our mother-in-lieu. We left.

III   *Les Deux Magots.*   I am twenty-four and free,
now, to finger knives and glasses—no cloth
to be stained, nothing but cold zinc dividing
me from your old friend opposite, your coeval
the Fugitive convert who cases the loud café
evasively while I lay my cards on the table:
I tell him of myself, which is as much
as to have asked him pardon—Shakespeare, no less!—
but he winces at what he hears, and what he sees:

your Montparnasse is dead, my Saint-Germain
dead-set against the capital of gayety
you shared in the Twenties. Gay it is, though,
and so am I, to his disparagement
expressed, dear Hart, in terms of our *decadence*
as the flaming creatures pass. "Such men," he says,
"fare best, as we Southerners say of foxes, when
most opposed—none so spited by their own,
and yet I see how proud these sick cubs grow!"

There is a silence, colder than the zinc
between us. Hopeless. I have lost heart,
as I always do when I rejoin the Fathers,
lost the pride of my "proclivity",
and the penalty and disgrace of losing is
to become part of your enemy. Have I lost you,
Hart? I need you here, quarrelsome, drunk
on your permanent shore-leave from the opposite sex,
opposing shore, the loss, the losses, the gain . . .

There is always a chance of charity when we are dead.
Only the living cannot be forgiven.

IV   *Sands Street Bar & Grille.* At thirty-four
I am older than your ghost I follow in
under the Bridge that hisses overhead.
Dark enough here to make ghosts of us all,
and only a great layer of ghosts knows how
to be democratic in the dark: no wonder
you gave your hand to Walt, always on edge,
on the beach of embarking, the brink where they fall
into the sea, these castles of our misconduct . . .

Your ghost, anonymous, cruises among ghosts,
our neighborly disgrace. Was it from this
you made your Bridge, reaching up to Walt
and down to me—out of this River, this Harbor,
this Island and these, these sexual shadows, made
an enviable failure, your dread success?
I do not believe in exceptions—if you did it
then it can be done; show me your toys, ghost,
show me your torments out of which you rise,

dripping in your bones, from death to be
a trophy of disaster. What did you learn,
steeped in the great green teacher of the gradual,
when all you knew was sudden, a genius in need
of a little more talent, a poet not by grace
but the violence of good works? I still do not
understand you, but I stand under you here,
marvelling at the shadows where apprenticeship
is not vocation, of course, only voyeurism.

Albatross, siren, you haunt me far from home.
It is dark. Here not seeing is half-believing.

v *Garrettsville.*   By forty-four I know
   your beginning *lost at land*, your end *at sea:*
   sometimes beginnings can be more desperate
   than ends, patrimony more than matrimony,
   and middle age the worst despair of all.
   I do not find you here, or in the bars,
   or Laukhuff's, or that yellow restaurant—
   not even on the beach you walked with Walt,
   hand in hand, you told him: *never to let go.*

   But that is where you find me. Take my hand
   as you gave yours to him. We suffer from
   the same fabled disease, and only the hope
   of dying of it keeps a man alive. Keeps!
   I press your poems as if they were Wild Flowers
   for a sidelong grammar of paternity.
   We join the Fathers after all, Hart, rejoin
   not to repel or repeal or destroy, but to fuse,
   as Walt declared it: wisdom of the shores,

   easy to conceive of, hard to come by, to choose
   our fathers and to make our history.
   What takes us has us, that is what I know.
   We lose, being born, all we lose by dying:
   all. I have seen the Birthplace—a strange door
   closes on a stranger, and I walk away.
   Soon the shadows will come out of their corners and spin
   a slow web across the wallpaper. Here
   is where you met the enemy and were theirs.

   Hart, the world you drowned, for is your wife:
   a farewell to mortality, not my life.

5

Randall Jarrell
An Introduction to the Study of his Work

for Peter Taylor

. . . I am he that was
Tiresias:
whatever I have known is no more than
the half of knowing.
I am going
to tell you my dream: it is a blind one,
as all our dreams are
when we make war
into peace at the price of the body.
I came to myself—
to mind, a kind
of memory—in a dark wood where three
roads ran to and from
their trivium.
Here serpents were coupled into a coil
they could not uncouple,
incapable
of escape, for loving we cannot tell
or else cannot tear
from each other
what is not ourselves. I did what men do
in the presence of
unpossessed love:
I drove my staff between them, and even
as the blow fell, I
was a woman.
Then for nine months I knew another life
until I returned
upon myself

in the wood, when my time was upon me.
    But the snakes this time
        were in combat,
striking at each other. I did what women do
    in the presence of
        what possesses
life to do violence to itself: I lay
    myself down between
        them, and even
as the venom struck twice, I was a man.
    I am he that was
        Tiresias . . .

The Assignation with Valery Larbaud

Grand Hôtel de l'Europe et de l'Amour?
Not in Paris. I shall not meet you here.
Cafés in the Rue Madame have carried
conventionality too far (farther
than the eye can reach): Frenchmen see merit
in each return to *this* reality—
to realism, they call it. In the mere
fact of not lying, they see poetry.

Nor in unseasonable Vichy, where
a hand that rocks your cradle rocks your grave.
Boulevard Larbaud! You lived here too much
in hope of becoming a memory,
and you have. A becoming memory,
of course, for all your proprietary
ways with a minor spring, too many tin
Zouaves in the Thébaïde: clinical baroque.

Nor even on the last Blue Train, hard pressed
between the anonymous and the communal.
I'm warmer, though, working south, thanks to you—
Barnabooth gave us the new gospel, John
of the Wagons-Lits: *there are no diseases,
there are only patients*. The window steams;
I understand. When truth has no further
utility, it becomes a landscape.

Licit or not, our one good moment is
Likely to be in Alicante, there
on the mosaic sidewalk, watered down

for a mile each morning. I drink and watch
people walking past in white shoes, enjoying
themselves as much as if they were not English.
Here you come, on time of course, heading right
for our table, *Life and Habit* under your arm,

and the first thing you ask is, "are there not,
perhaps, too many English words which must
be rendered by *dont?*" There are, there are, and I
cannot meet you on your own terms; I cannot
bear you on mine. We laugh at that in Spanish
—laughter, the nervous substitute for awe—
and keep our eyes where they belong, across
the brilliant promenade, the yacht-club roof

with the best view of the harbor, the black
frond of Elche on the right . . . Prodigal sons!
Is there another kind? I keep watch for
some dark lieutenant from the sea, and you
—you vanish: ugly, forbearing, sad. Words
are eternal, but they tire so quickly.
You left me with Satan's: *Not to know me
argues thyself unknown.* I know you now.

Again for Hephaistos, the Last Time
October 1, 1973

. . . *translate for me till I*
accomplish my corpse at last.
W. H. AUDEN

What do we share with the past?
Assurance we are unique,
even in shipwreck. The dead
take away the world they made
certain was theirs—they die
knowing we never can have it.

As each of *us* knows, for even
a nap is enough to confirm
suspicions that when we are not
on the scene, nothing else is.
Call it the comfort of dying:
you *can* take it all with you.

"The ship is sinking": Cocteau managed to stage his whisper
while a camera was "well trained" (according to Stravinsky)
on the televised deathbed in Paris some dozen years ago;

his sparrow had fallen one day before this master forger
(who was hardly your *miglior fabbro*, although you had
        translated
his tangle of true and false Ginifers into your own
        Tintagel)—

finding Piaf had "gone on", as she always did, ahead
of time and tonsillitis, how could *he* help finding, too,
the vessel on the rocks, the wreck within easy reach?

10

Predeceased, your gaudy predecessor in death gave up
the ship—high season for sinking: Harlequin Jean, escorted
or just flanked by MacNeice and Roethke, alien psychopomps.

Yours though were quite as unlikely, every bit as outlandish.
This weekend, waves of applause (prerogative of popes!)
broke in the wake of a coffin leaving Santa Maria

sopra Minerva—Magnani, with Pablo Neruda your peer
on Sunday's appalling front page, though scarcely your pal:
Verga you loved, but had you stayed up late enough to see

"Mamma Roma" in his *Lupa?* Even heard of her? Like most
performers—like Piaf—she was, I suspect, as absent
from your now immortal reckonings as Rod McKuen et al.

You were not very fond of volcanoes—in verse or voice either,
and to violent Anna preferred a predictable Donna Elvira
who could always repeat her crises on key, on cue, encore!

Cocteau, you conceded, though stagy, had the *lacrimae rerum*
     note,
but did *you?* The *Times*, this morning, declared you had
     failed to make,
or even make your way inside, "a world of emotion".

I wonder. Given your case, or given at last your encasement,
who knows? Only the poems, and to me at least they speak
     volumes:
your death makes a leap-day this fall, this autumn you would
     say.

But my *personal* knowledge is odd, my evidence suspect even:
on a club-car up to Cambridge, two freshmen scribbled a
     note—

11

"Are you Carl Sandburg?" "You've ruined," you wrote back,
    "mother's day."

Was that emotion? Was this—the time backstage at the Y
when impatient to read to the rustling thousands out front,
    you asked
(possessing no small talk—and with you I possessed no
    large)

why it was I no longer endured a difficult mutual friend.
"Because he calls everyone *else* either a kike or a cocksucker,
and since, Wystan, both he and I are . . . well, both of
    them . . ."

"My *dear*," you broke in, and I think you were genuinely
    excited,
"I never knew you were Jewish!" No, not a world of
    emotion—
say, for the time being, as you said, the emotion of a world.

Only those poets can leave us
whom we have never possessed.
What did you leave me? The unsaid,
mourning, hangs around me,
desperate, not catastrophic,
like a dog having a bad time.

The difference, then, between
your death and all those others
is this: you did not take
a certain world away, after
all. After you, because of you,
all songs are possible.

Audiences

"A poem in which it would be impossible for a reader to be distracted from its personal relevance to himself by thinking of Goethe or, even more mistakenly, of me . . ."

W. H. AUDEN

1831

. . . Herr Wemyss (thanks to Ottilie) was then and there
    announced;
I left off my petrology and limped downstairs to receive him,
offered a chair politely but in pantomime: he had
no German, as he announced himself, cool as quartz;

so he sat down, and opposite him down sat I.
Wemyss was silent. I was silent. Hence we sat
silent both, together. Whereupon, after some
centuries or perhaps mere decades of smiling,

I stood up and he stood too, with one accord.
Again in pantomime, I took my leave of him;
he did the same, of course, and I accompanied
my stone guest to the door, although I dared not let

him leave without a word—my conscience (I too endure
my stony moments) was adamant there. Indicating
Byron's bust, I very slowly said, "that is
a bust of Lord Byron." "Yes," quite as slowly he replied

(in the same tongue, which was his own), "he is dead."
With this departed, I vow, my definitive pilgrim,
the dullest Briton of them all. Outside the door
imagine my astonishment at glimpsing on the road

a large pale fragment of—surely—Silesian schist!
"Now how did you get here?" I asked, an inquiry
my visitor, lingering, appeared to find quite lunatic.
I retired, in some distemper, to my study upstairs:

I cannot answer, as yet, for the presence of such schist
here in the dust of Saxe-Weimar-Eisenach, nor for that,
be it confessed, of the loquacious Herr Wemyss, after all
a compatriot of Lyell, of Bacon and Burnet and Smith! . . .

1971

. . . Tea? Until five we have tea. There's only powdered
      milk:
I find it does quite well. Was that the phone again?
Do start, I'll be back in a moment . . . Sorry, that was
rather an important call. Sometimes it can't be helped.

Now, whatever took you so far out of the proper path
as to be translating French? Of course you do it well
enough, but none of them will do *you* any good:
Perse? Chazal? Cioran? Of course, they're foreigners—

not French, Parisian—hence they translate so nicely, or you
      do.
The only one since Pascal who appeals to me in Frog
is—guess! No, Baudelaire. And Sainte-Beuve may be right
about him: it would have been better—*better form*, that is,

to do it in Latin. Which reminds me—choosing Latin does—
you must let up on that prose of yours. While you can, I
      mean:
affectations harden. Oh yes, Colette too, of course,
but her books are like some of their wines—don't travel well.

Women don't, as a rule, you know: very poor travellers.
It's because they can't pee in the sink. Simply can't do it.
No use being a writer unless you offer praise. Lacing-in
may be good for style (though I don't think it's good

for yours, my dear), but so bad for character. For example,
Stravinsky: you can't take revenge in words, the one revenge
to take is writing music. No more of either now:
he's gone, poor dear. At last. That's what my call was about.

Why write unless you praise the sacred places, encounters
when something is given over, something taken as well?
Five yet? We may permit ourselves a drink: to him.
The sacred and the suburban often coincide. You're
      leaving? . . .

Envoy

I am Herr Wemyss, of course, and Weimar is St. Mark's
      Place.
Such audiences tend to hold their own—they loom
against the light of memory, darkening, deepening, dire:

Auden mourning Stravinsky, Goethe speaking to stones.
For things to have a shape they must include a death.
The smell of a glass nearly emptied, stronger than when it is
      full.

(I I)

Semi-Private
Bay 12-13, Mount Sinai Hospital

for Hortense and Curtis Harnack

We share nurses and nausea where
no underhand move to make love
or commit suicide avails: the Pavilion of
Intensive Care

gets, and keeps, the upper-hand part
of our Magic Molehill—a bay
unruffled save for bells, themselves muffled to say
Be Still My Heart.

Faded blue draperies divide
us with a dyed fall, a dim Veil
of some Temple hiding what lies beyond a pale
we both abide,

being loath to commit, as well,
the minor sacrilege of speech.
I hear you sighing though—near enough within reach
for me to tell

each time you take another turn
for the worse, a *tour de faiblesse*
extemporaneous but punctual nevertheless,
as I discern

by peeking through—the seams are worn,
the stitches gape, and there you go
again, studying your outspread palms as though
you hoped to learn

what their literal manuscript said.
Lines-of-life are not in your line,
I predict: you are under age (you are half mine)
and yet half dead.

After a week of keeping score,
no body can keep a secret:
you leave a gallon jug the color of bad claret
on the tile floor

beside my own humble offering
of what looks like better sauterne;
a nurse collects them both on "round-the-clock return."
Our differing

in this matter is the datum
which keeps our silent partnership
solvent: we cannot give each other more than the slip,
and do not come

to grips with our opposite ills.
Nothing given is welcome here,
even when it gives up; what counts is keeping clear
count of the pills,

the pulse, and the pressure. No one
finds our cause catching, although
sufficiently uncommon to keep us caught: they know
how it was done,

not what it will do. Visitors
resent each of us, vaguely, for
the other's sake, and we resent them all—one more
mistake, of course,

in the unmistakable chain
of grievances; we even make
trouble for the pretty intern who comes to take
an hourly stain

of blood she bunches like tuberoses
(there are real roses, too, as bright
as anyone's blood, though nowhere near so up tight).
Diagnoses

alter . . . falter. Keeping pace with
the body is a handicap race;
once they deduct our identity from our case,
life is a myth.

Personal Values

My dear Magritte, I have been ill. Again.
By now of course the symptoms are well known,
Signs which are taken or mistaken for
Wonders by the broken-winded mind, blown
Is the word all right, though all wrong is more
Like it: blown up and at the last gasp down
Until I cannot call my soul my own

During such uncalled-for occasions when
The torn mind turns into the body, then
Turns out, instants or ecstasies later,
To have been literally taken in.
Taken—was it always as well known—where?
You know, but you're not telling, not even
Telling tales out of school—André Breton

Himself could never persuade you to own
Up to what he called your "magic reason":
You refused to tell tales *in* school either.
In any case or, to be casual, in mine,
Each time the fit approaches, I repair
(To be fitted, you might say) to the one
Room there is no earthly obligation

To share, the place in which to be alone
Par excellence, par misère, a site no one
Has named properly because it must pair
The washing function with the wasting one,
Lore of the toilette with the toilet's lair.
This is where the thing chooses to come on,
Yet once I get inside, the room has gone,

Nowhere to be found: the four walls open
Up and away—the sky! Against which, seen
As if for the first (or last) time, appear
The comb in the corner, the soap near the green
Toothbrush glass, one huge matchstick on the floor
Where Marie must have missed it, all obscene
With enormity, much too big to mean

What the scale of mere habituation
Managed to confer upon them or shun
By not conferring. I wait for my seizure
With the patience of . . . a patient, at pains
To discover the glass beyond me, over
My head, the soap escaping by design,
The totem matchstick—like the comb, a sign

Of my illusions made illustrious: icon
And idol, texts of a new religion.
As I wait for the next spasm to spare
Or despair, dear René (which means *reborn*),
I send all my thanks for your more than fair
Copy of my condition. *Merci*. Where
Else could I find my life's illustration?

From the Files of the Secret Police
Confiscated Material

Better burn this, my dear, should it ever
reach you. Their procedure here
(which accounts, I am sure, for their success)
is to let no one
whisper to the World Outside
the truth about life in these dominions,
or about death, certain deaths . . .
But so tempting was their offer, and so
flattering the terms
that offer was tendered in,
perhaps I accepted precipitantly,
unaware, once my qualms were
quieted, how real the jeopardy was—
you know how I am
when it comes to your comfort!
And though I long to tell you All, of course—
why else would I be writing?—
I see no purpose in paying the price
customarily
exacted for such "treason";
that, incredibly, is what they label
even the mildest impulse
of a mind to question . . . For my sake, then,
put this in the fire.
What, for instance, became of
that poor devil my predecessor here?
During our lessons, keeping
my voice quite steady, I did manage once
to ask the Princes,
but I doubt if they ever

so much as wondered: all that the boys know
      (for they are boys still, in spite
of the preposterous privileges
         they enjoy) is that
    he failed, one day, to turn up
for no particular reason, and that by
      the following morning's class
he was of course *replaced*—the opposite
        of the usual
    scholastic situation:
according to their practice in these halls
      the pupils are stationary
and the masters succeed one another—
        provisionally;
    now it is, simply, my turn.
However, this being their festival
    season, our lessons today
were suspended, the Court, like all the rest,
        eagerly taking
    part in their terrible Games
(as they call them), and even from this far
    away—holed up in an odd
corner: no one would think to find me here—
      I can tell the cries
    of the victims (not the ones
under the knife, but those waiting to go)
      from the continuous roar
of the "players", my dear, who have not yet
        had their fill of blood.
    Without, therefore, my functions
to attend to, and the Princes attending
    to *theirs*, it seemed the one time,
or never, to pry beyond these precincts
      apportioned to me.
    So this morning, at the mere
start of their madness, I left my lodgings

(too near the noise, anyway,
to be tolerable) and walked, unobserved,
past the ancient gates
of one of their Sacred Places,
the echoing yards quite empty today—
"today is for Sacred *Acts*,"
they would say, cutting down the next captive—
and saw there a thing
worth the risk of this message.
It must have been used a hundred times, yet
ready to serve all over
again, waiting in that abandoned shrine
for its one moment.
I looked at it a long time.
A proper account, and you should conceive
what these people are, beyond
all their talk of "Royal Tutor and Scribe"—
as if my duties
and my performance of them
somehow made what is happening right now
in the arena less real
or even less repellent. But there is more—
if I make you see
the necessary *beauty*
of the . . . beast, as well as its brute nature,
you will realize, perhaps,
why I remain here despite the dreadful
danger to us both—
not for gain alone, but grateful
to some long-lost savagery my life had lacked.
Try to see, to imagine,
then, a Pig longer than a man, a woven
hull of bulrushes
plastered over in long stripes,
grey, flesh-pink, ochre. Cowrie-shells for eyes,
tusks of ivory curving

back to the tufted ears which, like the tail,
   are worked from inside,
  their "practitioner" concealed
by a thick fringe of black straw. In the snout
  an obscene balsa-wood tongue,
and under its tail-whisk the testicles
   (two nutshells) neatly
  stowed, and the man inside it
becomes, when he stands, the missing member—
  dismembered now, while they are
at their killing, remembered later on
   when the rites begin
  and such "Pigs" devour the dead,
the great hulls squatting down on one body
  after another—can you
credit me when I not only assert
   but insist there is
  a reason in their ravening,
in their seasonal glut a loveliness,
  my dear, for all its horror?
You are the first, and by that primacy
   imperiled, to hear
  of these gory sacraments—
scarcely believable, yet they are so.
  Do not condemn too quickly
what I shall try to explain in my next.
   Meanwhile memorize
  these notes I dare not preserve,
for even now a stillness from the stadium
  means I must stop. Pay
our "messenger" well and, as you love me,
   destroy this. I shall
  return now to my Princes,
though our next few sessions promise to be
  unruly. I am quite well
and safe, so far. Next summer we may . . . not . . .

Howard's Way
A Letter to 102 Boulevard Haussmann

Mon cher maître, could even you have mastered
such dissemblance?
                    Given your gift for luring
the accidental and the inevitable
to lie down together, what would you have done
with these disparities—could you have parsed them
into a semblance of sense?
                    Mind, that phoenix,
kindles its own fire: identity at stake,
it does not depend on the world for fuel—
must I? Dear Marcel, did you?
                    Suppose I rehearse
how it went with me last night, how far it went
beyond my means: I write what I recover from
what I have chosen to forget. I put it
to you—perhaps you can put it right for me.
No one knows the ropes better, what lines to draw,
what chords to strike, what strings to pull—and knowing,
for better or worse, would tell.
                    Now just suppose
you had accompanied me, had paid a call
in answer to a call, a summons from hell—
as any place is hell, at the other end
of a telephone wire, that is not heaven.
Suppose you approached, with *your* urbanity,
my city's most publicized apartment-house
looming grim at the Park's edge, grimy and grand—
sufficiently grand to be used for shooting
horror-movies.

(I know, you cannot have heard
of horror-movies. Or can you? *Fantomas*
was shown in Paris, you saw *Judex, La Proie* . . .
Seeing is believing—we are what we see,
and if what we see and believe is silly,
only what we could see, could believe is not.)

Horror-movies then, and there—could you believe?
in the redoubt Dakota, so huge our word
apartment takes on a meaning all its own,
the converse of togetherness (now that word
you never heard of, thank God. We mean well, but
the ease with which we say what we mean—horrors!
sounds like the most affable of lies).

                           To the dark
Dakota then you came, suppose, and instead
of visiting its most Proustian denizen,
the leading lady famous not for her roles
but for her first appearance in a Southern
hamlet, also the birthplace that very year
(and the hideout since) of the one novelist
we've had who takes after your own hidden heart—
though knowing another man's secret is not
the same as having to live with your own . . .

Suppose, then, rather than visiting "the girl
next door" to our great fabulist, you had found
yourself and me outside another door, one
to an attic room, really a *chambre de bonne*
(more likely, in the Dakota, *de mauvaise*)
bestowed by that lady on her kissing kin,
the man who called us, whom we are calling on!

He famous as well: the poet-pornographer
freshly returned—restored—a pilgrim from Nepal
and beautiful, still beautiful, or worse still

you could see that he had been beautiful once.
He admits us, the old beau, with a hard look,
as though wondering how much we cost. (*He* cost
a lot, and can afford to be entertaining
only to strangers: entertainment at best
is merely lust compassionately disguised
as the will to please.

          Master, you *are* helping!)
Pattering across the parquet, his blind pug
attacks. "Down, Principe, down! Oh dear, do mind
that pile of poo." We bestride the pool of pee
by inches, whereupon we are well inside
a room filled (or emptied) by a flickering
blue light. There are others here, oblivious
of Principe and us: all their faces turned
one way, washed by a reflected radiance—
mysterious little male presences, looking
just like pressed flowers.

          We sit down too, we watch.
On the screen, persons inconceivably wound
around each other commit by noose and knout
actions of ecstasy and passions of pain
on a hairless Oriental boy, a child!
though is that a child's body? relentlessly
acquiescent to the penetrations of
a grey-haired man . . .

          All at once another man,
corpulent, with the face of a polite snake
(the man who uses all the instruments) comes:
there is a sudden struggle, until both men . . .
The child's hand flutters, though they hold him down, and
two fingers thrust across the screen in protest
or appeal: black talons, inches long.

          No one
speaks. Not a word. Only the reel chatters on—

the bodies exchange a last seizure, comic,
anonymous. To forego identity
as these do, first give up the fear of falling—
most of us cannot, for who would need to rise
if we were not afraid of falling?
                              By this
light or lack of it, the little audience
has the look of men watching and unaware
we are watching them watch: a look as though
they were not in their own bodies, but in ours . . .

Something breaks, the screen goes blank, and here we are
sitting with a dozen men in a room so
nondescript no reasonable person could
possibly make love here, or commit suicide:
keeping up appearances is not difficult
once you have seen through them—you told us, master,
merely hold them from behind, the way you hold
a shield, and appearances protect you quite well.

Introductions follow: the guest of honor,
a tall, grey-haired man of ash and addictions
whose first forbidden book everyone devoured;
the later licit ones are, of course, unread:
the one way we can survive is to become
imitations of ourselves—for otherwise
experience touches us and we must change.

Beside him, his sarcous secretary whose
pale eyes are so wide-set that like a serpent
he can look straight ahead only by turning
his face from side to side.
                              And across the room
a third person is identified, though hardly:
a living idol, fourteen perhaps, and so
symmetrical he need not have a self . . .

         "This

is Inda, I brought him back from Katmandu."
I hold out my hand as he does, the idol does,
and then I feel the nails. So he is the child,
those are the men—he suffered, they were there then,
here now: grey hair, snake-eyes . . .

         Horror-films, indeed—

we take off our sex and have . . . clothes! I cannot
bear this. Master, is art the image of life?
Is life?

      "Act your age," you urge me and, outraged,
I answer: "What is acting? I should act yours,
you mean—one more obscene performance . . ."

         You

take your part by holding your peace. You are not
there, you are silent—have you left me?

        Rudely,

I admit, I stumble, almost running, out,
unready for that recognition scene . . .

        Down,

away! where winter opens the clouds above
the Park and beyond the trees. There are the stars,
unsteady constellations—blue movies all
right, or all wrong: a world whose beauty is just
a jangle to our ears, a blur in our eyes,
an entanglement about our feet . . .

        I move

by darkness as *they* moved by light: Howard's way.
Crossing the city to send you this, I am
awed as the meanings converge, syllables
I cannot dispel, alien oracles
I cannot receive: Dakota. Katmandu.

        Richard

Compulsive Qualifications

for Stewart Lindh

I   *"Richard, May I Ask a Question? What Is an Episteme?"*

A body of knowledge. As I know best now,
Regarding yours across the abyss between
    That chair and this one,
My ignorance the kind of bliss unlikely
To bridge the furniture without a struggle,
    A scene—mad or bad
Or just gauche. The known body is Greek to me,
Though I am said to have conspicuous gifts
    As a translator.
More likely the Bible is the right version:
All knowledge was probably gained at first hand
    And second nature;
To know the Lord was to be flesh of His flesh.
There was a God, but He has been dismembered;
    We are the pieces.

II   *"Richard, May I Ask You Something? What Is a Two-part Invention?"*

The sense of invention is a coming-upon,
A matter of finding matter more than of fact,
     So that the finding matters.
And if invention is finding, all finding is
Finally choosing, and a choice is something made.
     Hence the sense of our saying
We "make" each other: because we choose that body
Over and above this one (ours), coming-upon
     Becomes more than just coming,
Becomes rather a coming-to, and to . . . ourselves.
Now in a two-part invention, the choosing works
     Both ways, we exchange our parts
So we can be found by each other, and coming
Together, coming apart, not even coming,
     We shall have been invented.

34

III   *"Richard, May I Ask You Something? Is Poetry Involved with Evil?"*

If we follow Sade (as we do, from a distance—
After all, who could keep up?) the Law is crime's cause,
      Wedlock the source of divorce,
Nor can any Garden grow till we acknowledge
The weeds suffered outside, not sadistically,
      Just dialectically.
So much, then, for "involvement": no *Paradiso*
Without, in poetry at least, infernal parts.
      But let the word itself speak—
Evil, from Indo-European roots, flowers
Like a weed, meaning "up-from-under" and "over"
      (as *eaves* drop from above us),
Meaning also "supine", "thrown-backward" and "under",
Meaning, as roots so often seem to mean, its own
      Opposite besides itself.
There we have it, as *I* would have it: infernal
Parts beside themselves, opposites supine, so that
      As even this four-letter
Old-English word means, *we* can be "extended forms
Which signify *exceeding the proper limit*."
      Flowers of excess—O good!

IV   *"Richard, Isn't There a Good Movie We Could Go Out To?"*

Out? I keep going in to mine, the blue kind
You come in the middle of. But then, you are
     Color blind, and not to blame.
Your memory for figures must be as bad
As a mirror's, or is it too dark in here?
     The best features have moved on:
What merely happens passes, and what never
Happens is eternal—perpetual motion
     Pictures. Camera! Action!
It *is* a good movie I am watching here
In which I began as its only actor, end
     As its only audience.

v   *"Richard, We Were Here Before, Don't You*
Remember?"

I remember how the valley turned from umber
to burnt sienna, how the clouds above Siena
    broke their Tuscan habit
of harboring grudges—it came down that morning
as if nothing would be held or held back again!
    But we were never there.
I remember the road to Rocamadour turning
round until it was ready to make a run for
    the hills overhanging
a chateau caramel in the afternoon light.
I remember how you took one hand from the wheel
    and your new driving-glove
was the same caramel. You turned, like the valley
or like the road, and I remember your face then,
    but it never happened.
And your face now, now we are here and our hostess
shows us to the same table we shared last time
    in Ye Waverly Inn
—I forget your face. "Last time" is no more than lost,
a series of revelations leading up to
    a full-length mirror,
and only my fictions can free me from myself.
Liberation is never complete while life "lasts",
    and nothing afterward.

VI   *"Richard, May I Ask A Horrible Question? Isn't It*
     Painful When Two Men Make Love Together?"

There is a horrible answer, to part of it—when
two men make love apart, that is the most painful.
Remember what I say—it may come up again.
     But you mean something else:
bodies whose engineering has failed to manage
or match their architecture, in which case Power
gets no good out of Form, or only the better
     of Form. Is that what you mean?
There is a solution (*I* mean, it is soluble):
you concentrate upon the parts and let the whole
take care of itself. Anyway, what about pain?
     Is there pain and not-pain?
Or is there the discovery that they become
each other when you traverse a certain terrain?
It is like electricity, pain: not a thing
     but the way things behave.
Behaving yourself, then, is a way of having
yourself be; pain a manner (sometimes a Grand one),
not what is the matter. Merely signifying,
     it is insignificant.

VII   *"Afterwards, Richard, What Will We Do? What Will*
We Say?"

When you work the mirror over, prying for signs,
perhaps it will come as a surprise that there are
              none to be found in the glass.
What we do leaves no trace on others, what is done
to us, none on ourselves: so much for principles.
              Kissing is not cosmetic,
merely cosmic, and even after there has been
breaking and entering, everyone's flesh is opaque
              to the feelings of others.
A given body takes time, like a good burglar,
and cleans up after itself. Nothing our hands do
              discharges our heart's behavior,
yet the change will be there, you are right about that,
though wrong to look for it where you do: there will be
              no revealing scars—nothing
shows up except what is shown up to be nothing,
standing for what cannot be said or done now,
              or not standing for such things
another minute, representative but intolerant.
Before, what we did not do or say found its sense
              or subsistence—livelihood—
in the unlived life. From here on in, a likeness
alone remains, a semblance of the unspeakable.
              So little is to be learned
from our fashions of making love, even from passions:
our faces do not show the past, they face our fate.
              Every sentence has been earned.

VIII   *"Richard, May I Ask You Something? Does the*
Particular Spoil Things?"

All things speak names, by which they leave us.
Once I have learned, close up, what to call
the corners of your mouth, what label
attaches to the blue italics
under your eyes—once spoken, the names
      no longer apply.

Abstraction is the one property
that may be shared, the rest is only
impropriety. Nothing is "spoiled",
merely erased, by particulars.
As you teach me, what must be learned
      can be forgotten.

"Sort of" . . . "you know" . . . "like"—idiomatic
efforts to accord ourselves to the world
where one of a kind counts for nothing
      more than an unrequited
passion for things in general. A life
in which anything can happen is all
right, but what if nothing happens twice?
      Consider the freakishness
we fear in ourselves because it so much
fascinates us in others . . . Consider,
for instance, that bald man leaving the bar
      with you beside him, talking:
are they a genre, that pair? He listens
for more than you can be telling him—what
you have read is no excuse for what you say.
      You are young enough to take
care of yourself, though he must be young too:
he claims he is growing older. Still talking
round the revolving door, you walk outside
      under a sky corroded
by stars—a cold night boding a slow spring
to come. Is that genre? The two of you
reach the corner, separate into single
      figures among the many.
Who was ever an individual when
he was alone? We belong to states, kinds,
likenesses not ourselves. We are others,
      and others are all genre.

Seen too much—seen ill—our media enforcing
upon that face a commonplace extremity:
                hibernation all year round.
Say his contempt breeds our familiarity,
such ceremonious trifling as renews the old
                Teutonic myth of a cap
which renders its captive invisible to us,
his contemptuaries. How often have we heard
                the obvious old refrains?
Listen and be grateful. When greatness means being
able to grow old in a peer-group that parades
                eternal adolescence,
then repetition is a seemly tunic for
a man everywhere dismantled by the human
                envelope he wears like stone.
Let it not come as a shock but a saving grace,
if he should answer our hungry interviewers:
                "My dear, let them eat cock!"
Poets *should* be obscene and not stirred. It is their
own method acting up: making themselves public
                without making themselves known.

"Richard, Do You Mind If I Split?"

Enough to be of two minds about the matter,
unless it is the manner, of your going hence
     even as your coming hither:
ripeness is hell, if the way you lead up to it
or down from it is all there is likely to be—
     a question of enduring
each departure to prepare for each arrival.
I watch you at the start of our times together,
     lathered by onset-angst,
then subsiding into the solace that is my
easy gift, to patiently split infinitives
     or hairs or seconds, until
the old withdrawal symptoms bubble up again.
I have more than half a mind to say I do,
     because I want you to be whole,
but my parting shot must be a partial lie—white
or off-color, as you leave the room: "Of course not.
     Split. I shall be of one mind soon "

Of course: the Buss Fair! the Kiss Affirmative!
fervent device of some obsolescent lore,
                    (as though compulsory busing
had not become a commonplace business now,
a matter of changing, merely, who we are).
                    COUNT YOUR CHANGE. I am counting
mine, and counting on it, in fact. Beware,
plain though you may find the fare I can afford:
                    I mean it not to take you far,
needing a force to take you only further
in—necessary transformations, fortunes
                    reinforcing the affair.

No daydream: my invitation to the voyage
was issued on acceptable terms, our journey
taken after all; Tuscany lies behind us,
     and here we are. What is "here"?
We are in Orvieto—or virtually: downhill
and up the other side, in Abbadia, where
the ruins of Cistercian dedication stand
     but fail to stand for much more
than a first-category *albergo*,* *
for the dodecagonal belfry upstaging
a cast of stars awarded more liberally
     by May and midnight. Way up
there on its volcanic-tufa promontory,
il Pozzo di San Patrizio,* * as well,
spirals down a shaft deeper than ours is high to
     "water remarkably pure".
We walk around the Abbey property whose "pool"
is not yet filled for the season and whose pale,
by this massive darkness, we dare not pass beyond:
     the night-watchman makes his rounds,
a white Alsatian mild at his heels, but who knows?
We stand, pointing like our ruins to the Duomo
illuminated tonight for the likes of us—
     God's great barn, empty and bright.
And at this moment they begin, the nightingales,
so loud and so many that you touch me and ask . . .
Noise! The natural history of nightingales
     comes down to that! and from this:
"No bird hath so sweet a voice among all silvan
musicians: singing for fifteen nights together

when the leaves begin to afford them a shelter,
    with little intermission
or none. So shrill a voice in so small a body,
and a breath so long extended, alone in song
expressing the exact art of Music . . ." Sandys,
    Milton, Keats to Hollander's
Philomel, nightingales sing with no intermission,
but now, only now, tonight in Umbria, *a noise*.
Back there on the cliff the black-and-white cathedral
    glows, a glory at a glance:
our eyes answer to what they know, our ears to . . . noise,
the natural experience—and that is why
we can close our eyes and cannot choose but hear.
    In our adjoining rooms, light
from that created passion overhead spills in,
and nightingales persist, noisemaking undismayed
by a barking dog, a car braking, then a cry
    that rings out as if it came
from your room, or mine. Night and nightingales return
to ash, daylight sifting over our divided
beds, the Duomo gray against the dawn again: I
    grudge the midnight's easy gift.

XIV *"Richard, What Will It Be Like When You Ask the Questions?"*

Like a landscape by night, and in summer, riding
the ghost of a road (or what you take for a road,
wet still and hissing under your bicycle tires
        after an afternoon's rain),
but the ground keeps rising, the gray cumulus thins,
and there is the moon! round and sudden in the sky
like an old sun casting a sort of dead daylight
        upon the world's premises,
cancelling shadowy promises of escape
at a slowed tempo of resignation, so that
there is no story left to tell yourself or me
        about the Day that Never
or about the Night that Always—no story now
about what had been or what would be—it is how
you become a storyteller: there is no story,
        so you have to make it up.
Even the same actions differ when repeated;
this one will be the same, but with a difference
more interesting than the sameness, which is
        more significant than
the difference. You will find it matters little
whether noon or the false noon of moonlight fastens
your shadow to the macadam, whether you put
        questions or are put to them,
loser, you will find there is nothing to choose,
whether you make others suffer or prefer them
to inflict suffering on you: it is always
        a god being crucified.

47

Discarded

by the Central Falls Free Public Library
and discovered by me (taking the mean words
as they give themselves out: am I not central
to myself when I scour the margins? and free
falling, if not yet fallen free? and public
precisely in the library sense?), turning
up just when it had been turned down, discarded

by the Central Falls Free Public Library
then: REFERENCES FOR LITERARY WORKERS
with introduction to topics and questions
for debate, Chicago, 1884
(page 80 torn out, found October 13,
1929). So was I—one among
other facts which as such need no sense, data

like that detached page, lost the 45 years
of my life and found on "my"—someone's—birthday . . .
Adoption is that human act which alloys
accident and intention. Hence my saying
I was "found", come upon, invented—found in
nature and not yet imitated by man,
as the old poets used to speak of *invention*.

Here was the question put to this literary
worker, providentially asked of the *dopted*
I liked to call myself, on the page restored:
Has the prevalence of fiction in modern
literature been, on the whole, a good thing?
References follow to Helps' *Friends in Council*,
Hollander's *Every Day Topics*, Friedman's

On the Threshold, Thwing's *Reading of Books*,
Van Doren's *Mercantile Morals*, and a Miss Willard's
How to Win. Even Miss Willard, I wager,
will not help much, and Helps less, for the problem
on my pasted page, the question of fiction, is
not one of doctrine but opportunity.
We make coincidence the sign of ourselves,

provided it glistens with significance:
that lost-and-found leaf with the magical dates
becomes a page in my précis of process,
an event filled, even to overflowing,
with meaning—but meaning at large, not any
one meaning (to unify ourselves is, in
itself, a great mutilation; harmony

prevails in the soul only over ruins) . . .
The prevalence of lying—never to leave
the Masked Ball, never? never—*is* a good thing,
for nothing is true until we believe it
so well we know its being no longer lies
with us. It is to others we lie, and tell
(is this not one?) fictions only to ourselves.

(I I I)

The Giant on Giant-Killing
Homage to the bronze David of Donatello, 1430

      I am from Gath where my name
in Assyrian means *destroyer*, a household word
by now, and deservedly. Every household needs
a word for destroyer—nothing secret in the fact,
nothing disgraceful about a universal need—
      and my name is a good word.
Try the syllables on your on tongue, say *Goliath.*
It sounds right, doesn't it—powerful and Philistine
and destructive, somehow. It always sounded like that
to me. *Goliath!* I shouted, and the sun would break
      in pieces on my armor.
The world, as far as I could see, was the sun breaking
on things, making them break. So I was hardly surprised
when the world came to an end because the sun broke *through:*
no pieces, unbroken, whole—no longer flash but flesh.
      The end came as a body.
You see, I am past the end, or I could not know it:
look at my face under his left foot and you *will* see,
look at my mouth—is that the mouth of a man surprised
by the end of the world? Notice the way my moustache turns
      over his triumphant toe
(a kind of caress, and not the only one), notice
my full lips softened into a little smile. You see:
the triumph is mine, whatever the tale. And the scene
on my helmet tells the true story: a chariot,
      eight naked boys, wingèd ones,
and the wine, the mirror, the parasol—my triumph
inherits me. He holds my sword. He is what I see,
that is why you see him: the naked boy without wings.
There is a wing, but it happens to be my helmet's

and inches up the inside
of his right thigh stiffening to allow the feathers
an overture, covertly spread, to that focus where
nothing resembles a hollow so much as a swelling.
That focus?—those. Find one place on his fertile torso
    where your fingers cannot feed,
one interval to which all the others fail to pay
their respects, even as they take the light, the shadows.
It is why the sun broke through me that morning—no stone
could lay Goliath low. See it still in the boy's hand?
    No need for a stone! My eyes
were my only enemy, my only weapon too,
and fell upon David like a sword. The body is
what is eternal; the rest—boots, hat ribboned and wreathed,
even the coarse, boy's hair that has not once been cut—
    a brevity, accidents,
though it is no accident when it is all you have.
Almost I think his face too is an accident, dim
under the long pointed brim. Call it an absence then,
an absence where life is refreshed and comforted
    while the body has its way:
a presence, a proof emptied of past and future, drained
of obligations pending. Climb across the belly,
up the insolent haunches from which the buttocks are
slung (there, that is the boy's sling), scan the rhyming
    landscape of the waist between
the simple nipples arched by his simpler, supple arms—
even the vulnerable shoulderblades, the vain wrists
are present but not the face, not David's mouth that is
the curved weapon used to kill a smile. And the carved eyes,
    what are they seeing? Only
the body sees, the eyes look neither down at me nor
out at you. They look away, for they cannot acquit
what is there: the eyes know what the body will become.
It is why they are absent, not blind like mine, not blank
    as iridescent agates.

They see the white colossus which in eighty years will come,
unwelcome: marble assertion of a will to wound
against which no man or music can survive. It is
what giant-killers must become. Michelangelo . . .
      They become giants: no head
of Goliath kisses those unsolicited feet,
no one is there . . . Yes, I go, I have gone already.
I would rather mourn my going than mourn my David.
I am the man Goliath, and my name in Israel
      is also a household word,
every household needs the word—perhaps there *is* a shame
in that, a secret about such universal need—
but it is a good word, my name; try it on your own
tongue, savor the hard syllables, say *Goliath*
      which in Hebrew means *exile*.

And So The Prince Obscured His Contemplation

To earn what you have had
empty your hands of it

I write from their capital.
   I have pushed the desk
near the window, listening
   to lottery women
calling through the walls, cries
   of sailors at noon
when the port is crowded.

You cannot forgive pain
but you can forget it

This morning I was tortured;
   tonight, perhaps, too.
I can imagine the prayers
   offered, even now,
for my return; the ransom
   not offered—not yet.
The Cardinal will come soon.

Nothing is over
what is done remains

There are plans for my escape—
   our people are fools!
How could a cripple follow
   these roads, these rivers?
Even tie me on a horse—
   they would know of it
before I reached the bridge.

We travel to be there
for we are where we are not

Invisible the country
    I rule, I can be
only a servant, a beggar
    at the bolted door.
I leave combat to my son,
    and to my father
who connived to send me here.

                    Illness has a purpose
                    it is an attempt at cure

The bells of the steeples sound
    withered, and watchful
as I am not to knock down
    any number of them
with this elbow of mine, this knee,
    if I breathe too fast
the city will be destroyed.

                    We live because we dream
                    we speak because we act
                    we know because we do not know

Vocational Guidance,
with Special Reference to the Annunciation of Simone Martini

                    Ordinarily
        when the Messenger, otherwise known
            as the Angel, makes himself
known, the rest of life absorbs his arrival—
        or the rust of life;
                        not that we tell lies,
        but we shall always be in terror
            of the truth. Habitual
disorders suffice to hold fast to the small
        change of small changes:
                        the dog keeps doing
        undoable harm to the Bokhara,
            your mother has called, again!
and that letter from the bank is anything
        but reassuring.
                    Events are enough—
        what Baudelaire calls *la frénésie*
            journalière—to mitigate
an inopportune disclosure, to muffle
        Angelic demands.
                    For Mary herself
        the moment was unmanageable;
            according to old masters
the Virgin resorted to household effects,
        a dither of forms
                    in a minor world
        where whatever is the case is lower
            case, a means of avoiding
the garbled message: was it Give or Give Up
        Something Capital?

You know how it is.
Not yourself for days (we all have spells),
   you need *things* around the house
to help out—objects of *virtù* to shield you
   from the articles
         of a faith that goes
   against the grain of mere existence.
   With some degree of success
you make your way into the gradual warp,
   pleasant evasions
         in which the masters
   specialize, plastic as all get out—
   when there He is! utterly
demanding, utterly demonic, speaking
   unutterable
         truth *and* consequence
of truth. Disaster, even triumph—
   no matter what the Angel
says, it is the Angel saying it: how can
   that be anything
         but gibberish, how
can you bear it? Only by binding
   an extra strand of daily
confusion around your Messenger, turning
   text into texture,
         praise into no more
than prose, a general excuse for
   reading languidly between
the lines when an Angel pronounces your fate
   in brisk iambics.
         Mary was finding
her comfort in Deuteronomy:
   "With the smooth stones of the stream
is thy portion, there thy lot," when Gabriel
   lighted before her.
         Simone saw it,

and not all the plausible veneers
of Siena can rival
his unvarnished truth (though many times restored)
in the Uffizi.
It might be your life:
no vainglorious architecture
vaults into, no garden leads
your eye out of, the picture. Lilies, a bench,
and the two of them
up against flat gold
and cold marble—no getaway, no
domesticity, unless
you call the still-fluttering plaid stole knotted
at Gabriel's throat
a domestic touch.
Even the scarf draped behind
Mary can be misleading:
it looks more like wings, when wings are the last thing
in the world she wants:
wings are terrible,
they take up too much room, too much air,
they speak volumes. Gabriel
speaks only words, marring the gold but making
right for Mary's ear—
words are terrible.
No olive-branch he bears, no wreath
he wears can ease this meeting,
and Mary—Simone Martini's Mary,
you can see, abhors
her bright Intruder.
She was just . . . she *was*. Sulking now for
the rape of that imperfect:
"I was reading when I heard . . ." Why is he here?
Who needs an angel?
A glance at her hair
and Gabriel's (identical gold)

explains. It is Simone's
method, this auburn pun, his way of saying
　　we ourselves summon

　　　　　　　　　Angels. Unwilling?
　　Unready? Giving rise to second
　　　　　　thoughts . . . If it had been enough
to brood over books, she never would have seen
　　her Visitor;

　　　　　　　　　resentful, reverent,
　　Mary at this moment discovers
　　　　　　that she wills him to appear—
even the wings are part of her—no use tugging
　　the long blue mantle

　　　　　　　　　　away from the Good
　　Tidings into an almost abstract
　　　　　　or Japanese pattern of
refusal. Pay those bills, call your mother back,
　　and clean up after

　　　　　　　　　the dog: no dodging
　　the moment when you meet the Angel,
　　　　　　when he announces what you
have known all along. No second-guessing:
　　"Father, let this cup

　　　　　　　　　pass from me"—his words
　　must enter the porches of your ear,
　　　　　　hammer strike anvil, until
the choice you have made, as Simone shows,
　　　　　comes, unfurnished, home.

Venetian Interior, 1889

for David Kalstone

Stand to one side. No, over here with me:
out of the light but out of darkness too,
where everything that is not odd or old
is gold and subjugates the shadows. There,
now you will be no trouble and behold none—
anything *but* trouble, at first glance,
last chance to see what I say is worth a look.

This whole palazzo is the property
of a middle-aged and penniless dilettant,
Pen Browning (Robert's son), who has made terms
—palatial terms, in fact—with towering
premises afforded by the tact
of his New York heiress, Fannie Coddington
Browning, dutiful daughter-in-law, doubtful wife.

Yet who would not be full of doubts, perplexed
at having to define Pen's talents and finance
his tastes? Their Ca' Rezzonico itself
is dubious. The ripened fruit of centuries,
rat- and roach-infested, peeling, rank,
withers with each tide that rots the piles,
though apt withal to weather these tenants as well . . .

He is painting from the model: *Dryope*,
undressed of course but draped against the draft
in a looping swathe of silver-printed stuff
that seems to move, glistening over flesh—
it *does* move! lapped in its silver mesh are coils
of a python wrapped in loving torpor round
the *contadina*'s undistracted torso.

The afternoon is numb: Dryope sleeps
in her pose, the python slips a little
down the umber slope of her thigh, and Pen,
inspired, slaps a dashing curlicue
across his canvas. "I had the Jew come by
with this brocaded velvet yesterday—
I bargained some old clothes against it, Fan,

so you needn't ask how much it cost in dollars."
To whom does Pen speak, his eyes intent, his hands
"working busily"? Beyond his "subject", look
past the unimposing *Dryope*, look through
the tufts of pampas grass extending up
to the tufa vault whose patination casts
a pall of watery splendor on the scene—

if you manage to overlook the sumptuous junk,
jasper urns, a suit of Japanese armor,
two stuffed bears, on the divan bearskins too—
there, or in this atmosphere let me say *lo!*
on that very divan Robert Browning lolls,
a short and foreshortened colossus with feet of clay
but the hardest imaginable cranium, among

his son's possessions slightly ill at ease
though well bestowed on slippery pelts, and plays
(against the wealthy Fannie—see her white shawl?)
at draughts with agate pieces, red and green,
like a page from some old parchment of kings and queens.
In approbation of his son's economies
the old man smiles now—but does she? The skull

interfering with our view of Fannie is,
I believe, or was the Mahdi's which Pen keeps
beside his easel (Victorians could make
anything into a tobacco jar). "I took
my pipe through Cannareggio on a long tramp
yesterday morning, right into the Ghetto,
looking for likely faces, which I found!

Didn't you say, Father, a satisfactory Jew
is worth a dozen Gentiles? The one who sold
that velvet to me is sure to be ready by Spring:
for *Lear*, you know, or *Lazarus* at least . . ."
Pen chatters on to charm the python, not
Dryope or Fannie who look up
only when the poet, roused, exclaims—

as rapt before himself as a child in front
of the Christmas tree: "A satisfactory Jew!
Setting mere Rothschildsplay aside, Pen,
I never saw but one in all my life:
Dizzy, I mean—the potent wizard himself,
at Hampton Court a dozen years ago,
murmuring at the Queen's ear like a wasp

who hoped to buzz his way into the diamonds . . .
With that olive cast and those glowing-coal-black eyes
and the mighty dome of his forehead (to be sure,
no Christian temple), as unlike a living man
as any waxwork at Madame Tussaud's:
he had a face more mocking than a domino—
I would as soon have thought of sitting down

to tea with Hamlet or Ahasuerus . . ."
As if on cue, the poet's high voice fades,
the lights on his tree go out. Yet we have seen
enough and heard enough: the secret of losing
listeners—did Browning never learn?—
is to tell them everything. We lose details.
The Mahdi's skull and Fannie's coincide . . .

The scene blurs and the sounds become no more
than exaggerated silence. Stand with me
another moment till our presence is
sacrificed to transitions altogether.
Time will not console—at best it orders
into a kind of seasonable chaos.
Let me tell you, it will not take much

longer than a medical prescription—
I can give you ingredients, no cure . . .
Visitors to the palazzo used to speak
of the dangerous ménage—the menagerie!
Yet the Costa Rican python that cost Pen
(or Fannie) sixteen pounds was the first to go,
untempted by the rats of Rezzonico;

Dryope followed Dryope underground,
the girl carried off by a chill and buried
at San Michele, the great daub interred
in the cellars of the Metropolitan . . .
"Dear dead women, with such hair, too",
we quote, and notice that hair is the first
of ourselves to decay before—last after—death.

In a year Robert Browning too was dead, immortal;
in another, Fannie dropped her shawl and took
the veil and vows of an Episcopalian nun;
and Pen? Oh, Pen went on painting, of course—
buono di cuore, in yellow chaomois gloves,
obese, oblivious, dithering into debt
and an easy death. The sale of what we saw

or saw through in Venice *realized*, as they say,
some thirty thousand pounds at Sotheby's.
I told you: first glance is last chance.
Darkness slides over the waters—oil sludge
spreading under, till even Venice dies,
immortally immerded. Earth has no other way,
our provisional earth, than to become

invisible in us and rise again.
Rezzonico . . . Disraeli . . . We realize our task.
It is to print earth so deep in memory
that a meaning reaches the surface. Nothing but
darkness abides, darkness demanding not
illumination—not from the likes of us—
but only that we yield. And we yield.

The Comedy of Art

"*Ah, la vie!*"   HENRI DE TOULOUSE-LAUTREC

Like Hamlet you began at thirty handing out
Advice to the players; you too were in disgrace
With mother ("to be a proletarian, *mon fils*,
Is no misfortune—to become one, disaster!")
And welcomed a chance to choose your companions.
First you took theirs, advice coming straight from
The horse's mouth, as you were at pains to make clear:
Circus ponies, Polaire's *fox*, the Tabarin tom—
You took their mouths and gave them to Yvette Guilbert,
Over her protests which later on subsided
Into a resigned admission that "life knows best".

But you gave as good as you got, or gave as bad,
Making up for what you could not really make out
By making it up: you invented a theatre.
Presences were everything. What was around you
Was merely behavior, and you wanted conduct—
The wanting was action: you would be the needle
In their world of hay. You became a steel needle,
Covering the walls of Paris week after week,
And above you rose that other steel needle where
You gaily, daily dined: "one place I do not have
To see the Eiffel Tower is inside the thing."

Eccentricities you felt—painfully—because
You were at the center: every morning you gave
Your mirror a look of profound understanding.
No wonder you welcomed the players, wanting them
To feel as well as see the point: art is a sword,
Though in most cases the scabbard wears out the sword.

67

It started as a mystery of masks, whereof
You were the master, choragus, mage: amazing
Trollops, old men, lovers, you transformed them all,
Green-and-white Brighella, Polidoro, motley
Harlequin, the passionate Spaniard, and *Elles* . . .

If life is a battle, in yours there were two kinds
Of women: the spy and the nurse, hard and soft—
Jane the red witch with a snake around her hips,
Fat May who had to breathe through a mouth that was
An open secret, a blank check, though drawn only
Deformity deep. It was the incomplete you loved,
A promise that you would never exhaust yourself,
Merely your subjects. How many times you warned them
(Though only Yvette listened to you, and lasted):
The closer art comes to taking off, to improvising,
The more it depends on convention—taking on.

You depended (everyone sees it now) on all
The banal fatality of talent that could
Encircle anything but yourself, and dreaded
Not solitude in space but exile in time—
Against that you were as helpless as the others.
It meant an art of exasperation, nowhere
At rest, needing . . . And as for life, the eyes have it:
A real hell was always preferable to home,
That imaginary paradise. Torment, you learned,
Is the public's natural habitat: only
Saints have any capacity for happiness.

So there was generally a sombre Gentleman
Gloating round the edges while the footlights shed
A fishy glare upon the ladies: *fauve qui peut!*
How hard your vices were to you, and how hard
Your virtues to everyone else, we can see here:
Faces that tremble a moment after each smile,

Like the branch from which a frightened bird has flown
(Many have sacrificed who dare not give themselves).
What mattered was not to hold forth but back, or out:
Love, Messieurs, cannot be one (I quote Don Juan)
And love cannot be two (thank you, Narcissus).

Repeating yourself, you became original,
Spelled out in an alphabet of only A's:
Anguish, alienation and absurdity.
They called your nightmares ugly, grotesque, decadent!
You knew the things we steal from sleep are what we are—
Revelation, the pulled vision. What empire was
Ever destroyed from the outside? We generate
Our own barbarians, all suicides. At the end,
Suspicions confirmed, you dismissed the players
And found peace drawing, for Renard, the toad, the pig,
The bull, the goat, the snail, the dog—a few dumb lives.

Closet Drama:
An Aporia for Joseph Cornell

Any apartment lobby is a necropolis,
every dresser drawer a forbidden city—
so much you taught me, intimated, warned:
colors are trite, edges not to be trusted,
textures, behind glass, refuse to explain
a world where fate and God Himself have grown
so famous only because they have nothing to say.
The tiny is the last resort of the tremendous.

Toy towns, I guess you could call them, where
the toy has at last outgrown the child and faced
up to, or down, the fakery of its own function:
once it accommodates evil (by which I mean
change, others, time) the toy becomes art,
an idol. And we are all idolators, Cornell.
You made it seem easy enough to try. I tried
to worship with you, twenty years ago:

TO OBTAIN COLD WATER TURN HANDLE
INDIFFERENTLY TO LEFT OR RIGHT Now
this, I fancy, must be the sea, or
what you call the sea in such parts,
not having been, as you tell me, to
Brighton. For the ORGAN OF CORTI,
see under CORTI, as one might well
believe. Likeminded, our hostess
displayed her curious rash in a room
where His Eminence invariably slept.
At which he drew his sword, stabbing
as if to kill me, crying "Mad!" Oh I

screamed, of course, but the portals
closed ever so firmly upon him, his
shadow Never To Be Seen Again . . .
                                        No,

your method was no help to me, I lacked
the sustenance of legend, subject things
implicit in our lives so long that they turn
beautiful: a ball, a chart, the binding of
a smuggler's bible, the complacent zeal
of ivory opera glasses. Even in absence
these totems persist, persuade, The tombs
of temple prostitutes are object lessons,

and you have learned them: to the living, without
definition, but to you, each a thing in itself,
pregnant with sudden meanings, evidences of
the only god whose name we know, Mutation.
I cannot speak, while you can only show
the way to silence, wonder, awe. Voices die
out of place—writing happens to happen in time.
In your boxes, Cornell, time happens: there.

Purgatory, *formerly* Paradise

for Abby and Bernard Friedman, fellow travelers

He is used—these are his words—to wander about
in his pictures at will, Cardinal Bembo wrote,
perplexed but extenuating, to the Princess,
Isabella of Este, *so that what thing is*
in his mind may satisfy those who look at them.
What thing . . .
            The sun (is it the sun? the source of light
in any case, some definitive disclosure
seems by a sorcery to lie in stone, stuff, skin—
light falls from ourselves!) sinks behind us, suspended
in a visionary paralysis, almost
as if the proper spell, pronounced, would bring it back,
would keep the world at such a pitch of elegy
that looking is a kind of listening. Almost,
yet as *we* wander about, our shadows lengthen,
reaching to the right, though only here, close at hand.

Past this enclosure where we are, from cliff to cleft,
from what looks like the immovable Grand Hotel
on a far hill to the unmoved lagoon, nothing
darkens, nothing dies: it is the containing life
continuing Out There, forever beyond us.

I called this marble paling an enclosure,
this plain balustrade around a tessellation
(serpentine, carnelian, alabaster set
fast in a magical geometry that makes
radiant what is merely red and green and white),
but there is a gate down to the water lapping
beyond a low gray wall, and the gate is open.

We may go away—some of us are going now,
losing the light that was in us.

        Look to the left:
see him? Lowering as he leaves, maybe a Moor
in his silver haik and fur-trimmed caftan, going,
his face resolutely turned from us (toward Mecca?)
like some discarded hope, receding . . .

        Who is he?
Perhaps the elder brother—Gentile—who paints
for the Sultan in Constantinope. He goes.
The open gate lets us in and out, we are not
held captive here on our high terrace, we are free
to pray, unless we are holding a sword and scrip,
or unless our hands are tied behind our white back
so that the arrows in us become our prayers.
Are we praying, though, or playing? The naked boys,
babies but boys, explicitly boys, are playing
without a doubt. They are playing with oranges
gathered from a tree—for there is a tree here, though
its dark foliage seems to loom beyond the pale
that confines us—*that does not confine us:* we are
free, I tell you . . .

        The tree is confined, it grows
in a pot, stemming from its sinister chalice—
clay? stone? lead? who can say? Some substances elude
distinction: the unmelting pot stands pat, stays put
in the center of the starred pattern; more than that,
I think it is the center of the ringing world,
the omphalos of earth. You can tell from the tiles,
from the figure they form, that it is the Center.

One boy has shaken the tree, two others take up
the fallen oranges—he is still shaking it,
braced against the trunk, staring into the branches,
but his effort is fruitless, the fruit has fallen
to the . . . ground? no, to the warm mosaic granting

what Dante calls a place where all times are present.
On a pillow near the navel of the world (look,
even from here you can see it is green velvet,
that pillow, just as you can feel the tiles are warm)
sits another boy, golden as the naked three
but wearing a linen shirt. He does not look up
from the orange they have given him—even so,
judging by their gestures—determined, solemn, gay—
I know they will give him all of the oranges.

Everyone old enough to speak words is speaking
at once—praying, after all? Who is "everyone"?
Not yet to have named them is the weakness of our
wandering method—*in mediocritas res*,
as it were . . . Of the seven people with us, five
press their palms together, surely they are praying,
men and women both, old, young, and used to praying.
But not the man with the sword—he glowers after
the Moor whom more than likely he has driven off;
this man is angry, his red mantle shows as much,
and the great sword upraised: Saint Paul is not praying.
Near him and outside the balustrade but looking in
past his fervent hands, an old man in a gold robe
watches the children—no, he is watching the Child,
and if he is too old to be the father, it is
that kind of look: Joseph might come in through the gate
but does not. Job is inside, naked, white-haired
next to the white-armed Sebastian, also naked
but for the arrows. Their lips move, the old martyr's
and the young one's, but they stare, murmuring, across
the enclosure with no eyes for the glorious
selfish children—all they can see, through the branches
of the empty orange-tree, is the group of three
women.

Of course that throne catches the eye, carries
up four carpeted steps of fine-carved stone, carries
higher to the horn-of-plenty holding highest
a wonderful red parasol. It means nothing
to the woman in blue who does not know she sits
on a throne; she will not look up from her prayers,
she may not even know there is a woman, crowned
and crimson-gowned, kneeling on the step at her feet—
and Catharine looks up no more than Mary.
                                        Only
the woman nearest of the three—nearest to us
as we wander—looks at the children, at the saints,
at everything. She sees what we see. Her lips part
and she speaks out of her prayers—is she praying?
I think she has no place in this performance, which
is called a Sacred Conversation. Look at her:
she wears no crown, she stands aside in a white shift
under a black shawl. Surely she is not a saint,
not a virgin, not a child: she is what we are,
all the rest that widens out of faith (or narrows:
for us, faith is always at a disadvantage,
a perpetually defeated thing which survives
all its conquerors) into a gold, given world,
one without convulsive or aspiring moments,
one. Whereby it is elusive, Out There, beyond
our claims to grace or disgrace: eternal, profane,
a profanity at which she stares. We stare too . . .

The lake plays hide-and-seek with us, we find it there
pressing round the corner of its cliffs, turning cold
boulders in a childish, hushed, expectant way, and
we keep feeling its banks are too big for the lake.
Something lived here once, there are huge holes, doors, even
stairways cut out of rock down to the rising depth,
so that if the water repeats: *I take*, the rock
replies: *I give*.

A stone's throw across the channel
an anchorite, creeping out of his grotto,
stares knowingly at a startled centaur: life here
is a likelihood of life, call it a final
acceptance of monstrous possibilities, a world
where men—old men, old and tired—are not appalled
by such untoward encounters, but where myths are.
It is the one victory men win over myths.

Behind the centaur, under a wall reminded
by the light what even broken marble can be,
the goats are sleeping together with the sheep, while
their drover waits in his cave for the relenting
darkness; he stares into a gradual evening,
pondering no more than grass, maybe—green grass,
but a green that keeps a secret. The Cross up there
on the clifftop is no more to him than the centaur
trotting down the beach: for the goats, neither exists,
and the light has never heard of Jesus, only joy.

Farther on, further in, the prospect develops—
is that a town? At least the road starts there, curving
up from the lake where it leaves the ghost of itself
curving down, and life—what passes for life—passes:
another drover, someone with a donkey going
home, and a meeting between two human beings;
they are too far, or we are, to see more from here
than their meeting. They embrace: not as lovers do,
or enemies—just two human souls in a frank
community of pain. Then the road moves up, past
the sixteen buildings to the wilds.
                                        All this she sees,
the woman in black and white, bare-headed, alone.
And we see it, the world without a Sacred Book,
a world where neither the negligence of the rocks
nor the endless care of the waters can prevail,
but only that act by which a man wrests something

out of death he knows will return there, to its home.
Death is not home to us, even if home is death—
why else are we here, free on our frail balcony
while that world is bound in being? Patience is home,
and suffering and change, the pang of things past, the prong
of things to come. We bear our poverty within us.
Out There it is . . . out there: God stays in his machine,
and we—we breathe and live and are permitted here.

Longhi notes that *the trees brushed in against the sky*
on top of the precipice rising to the right
are a sixteenth-century addition. Who knows?
The inscription on the frame has also been called
a forgery: *Opus Ioannes Bellini.*

Richard Howard

Richard Howard was born in 1929 in Cleveland,
Ohio, and studied at Columbia University and the
Sorbonne. He is a distinguished translator from the
French and a critic of great versatility. His five
earlier books of poems are QUANTITIES *(1962),*
THE DAMAGES *(1967),* UNTITLED SUBJECTS
(1969), FINDINGS *(1971 and* TWO-PART
INVENTIONS *(1974) he is the author of* ALONE
WITH AMERICA: *Essays on the Art of Poetry*
in the United States since 1950, *and of the*
commentary in PREFERENCES, *a recent critical*
anthology of the relations between fifty-one
contemporary poets and the poetry of the past.